MW00873175

Find What's NEXT For You

Business Owners Share Their Transition Stories

by Steve Coleman and James Gambone

Foreword by Tom Hubler,
nationally recognized expert on family business
issues and CEO of Hubler for Family Business

Find What's NEXT For You
Business Owners Share Their Transition Stories

By Steve Coleman and James Gambone

Foreword by Tom Hubler, nationally recognized expert on family business issues and CEO of Hubler for Family Business

Cover and interior design by Wendy J. Johnson, Elder Eye Design, www.ElderEye.com

Copyright ©2015, Steve Coleman and James Gambone
All rights reserved.

ISBN 10: 1497582016
ISBN 13: 978-1497582019

Library of Congress Control Number: 2014913041

CreateSpace Independent Publishing Platform,
North Charleston, SC

Contact the authors at: www.Biz-Bridge.com

Dedication

To the courageous business owners and members of their families who have shared their stories of transition successes and failures at our breakfast roundtable.

Their stories continue to inspire us.

Contents

✳ ✳ ✳

Foreword

One of my favorite book titles is *A Little Book of Forgiveness*. The book you are reading could easily be entitled *A Little Book of Business Transition Wisdom*. What the authors artfully do is weave together a series of the personal anecdotes of entrepreneurs who are at the cusp of the biggest transitions of their lives. The book illustrates the complexities and wonder of their situations, as well as the impact of fate on the outcome of their transitions.

In addition to the stories, the authors weave in a series of helpful guidelines, tips, and checklists to assist the entrepreneur in the creation of his or her own legacy. The authors point out the importance of sharing your story when formulating your legacy. The wisdom that is generated in this book comes from listening to other entrepreneurs harvesting their life experiences, formulating their own stories, and presenting them to others.

Tom Hubler, nationally recognized expert on family business issues and CEO of Hubler for Family Business

✳ ✳ ✳

Authors' note

We have secured permissions from all of the owners
whose stories are used in this book. Because we didn't
want to reveal too much about the individuals or the
companies they own or sold or passed on, we deliberately
tried to provide only the sector they worked in and the
lessons they learned, while withholding proprietary
financial and other information. Who these owners are is
not as important as the lessons they were willing to share
with all of us.

INTRODUCTION
Planning When Life Is Calm!

By failing to prepare, you are preparing to fail.

Ben Franklin

This book is for and about business owners who are nearing the threshold in the next chapter of their business careers. As owners in the older generations have matured, we often hear, "Got the business covered. Now what about me?" Listening to owners tell their stories and helping them find a time, place, and voice to express these stories has been our labor of love for the last decade and more.

Owners believe the most valued source of advice isn't a consultant; it's another owner. So we started nine years ago hosting a monthly owners' breakfast roundtable—a safe place to share their transition stories. No two stories are the same, but the goals and paths forward have many shared realities. Rather than prescribe specifically how to go about a transition, we offer stories and lessons that often come from an uncomfortable, necessary threshold of change, and then move to place where an owner can begin to figure out for him- or herself what needs to get done.

We hope these stories will alert, inform, challenge, and provoke owners into action—to create a sense of urgency. If they do this, we know from experience that families, partnerships, businesses, and communities will be preserved and strengthened.

That's why *Find What's NEXT for You* is our passion and gift to business owners and their advisors. And as lifelong advisors and business owners ourselves, we want to walk alongside these entrepreneurs as they recognize that opportunities with new options are possible, even necessary, for the next stage of life.

Questions that emerge early in transition become driving forces as they are reflectively answered:

- **Where am I now?**

- **What if I have no idea about what to do next?**

- **What is next in my work?**

- **What should I do with the rest of my life?**

- **How can I leave a legacy that is an accurate reflection of my whole life?**

- **How can I avoid predictable mistakes?**

- **What is the best path for the next generation?**

- **How much can I do myself?**

- **What help might I need along the way?**

- **Who else should be involved in plans for the future?**

Through our years as advisors in business life, we know owners who have accumulated a wealth of many valued assets, both tangible and intangible. This abundance often leads to gratefulness, and that leads very naturally to generosity. We know that sharing what you have earned and learned can be the greatest gift of all.

The owners in transition we've met also wonder how they might use the deep business knowledge and personal relationships they've developed as they now enter a period after full-time business ownership. And they are concerned about their legacies after leaving their companies and about how they will be remembered by employees, their families, customers, suppliers, and the communities where they were doing business.

This book is a gift given to us, bit by bit, as owners have told and we have listened to their transition stories. And now we want to give you some of these same gifts—lessons of courage, longing, escape, fear of change, discovery, and amazing fulfillment that in some ways are not far removed from your earlier business and personal successes in life.

No two transition stories are the same. And yet we see familiar patterns—a flow, a sequence—as we move into later life. Usually, the

No two transition stories are the same.

first notion of moving on to a new stage in the journey is triggered by an unplanned event that befalls a friend or family member. One of the stories we heard involved a heart attack and surgery for a business-owning father at age seventy-seven. This triggered a long-overdue updating of the owner's will, the creation of a trust for grandchildren, and the development of a successor plan that took full effect fifteen years later.

There is a flow from vague awareness of inevitable change, to conscious thinking about the distant future perhaps ten or twenty years away, to active worrying for five or more years, to gathering fragmentary anecdotal information, to sizing up the best options, and to finally taking concrete action. Are you moving down this familiar path? Should you be?

In this practical book of real stories, we'll offer ideas that have proven effective and are based on real life in business and beyond. Each business and its owner deserve a unique strategy. Only the owner can be the real driver of this process. Maybe he or she needs the help of an "architect" who can personalize the direction, steps, and structure for adventures in life after leaving a full-time devotion to work life. Over the years, one reality stands out above the others: it is substantially better to work on transition "stuff" when life is calm.

Get-'er-done entrepreneurs have predictably strong attitudes about transition. "No rush. I can do this myself. It's simple. It won't take long," they say at the beginning. We offer some stories that start out this way and then

Particularly in times of chaos or emergency, people seem to want "the" answer to setting priorities in the form of a tool or method that they can apply to whatever situation they have to address at the moment. However, setting priorities is not something that is best done "in the moment," nor does it lend itself to a single or optimal method. While there are tools that can be used to assist, the fact remains that setting priorities requires you to develop a process that enables you to deploy your time and energy most effectively. Such a process can be planned ahead of time and followed as the need arises.

Pat Lynch, Ph.D., President of Business Alignment Strategies Inc.
www.businessalignmentstrategies.com

turn into a cascade of dominoes that need to fall in some reasonably predictable order. Maybe one or two of these stories will speak to you. We believe strongly in the value of spending time to think, question, gather opinions, and then decide when and how to move ahead with early steps of transition.

The second reality that stands out in our experience is that sustained transition progress is not a solo journey. You will benefit from the accountability provided by a trusted advisor who gently but persistently reminds you of the destination, the mile markers along the way, and the discipline needed to stay

Accountability by a trusted advisor, is an essential transition consideration.

focused and on track through good times and not-so-good times. The advisor might help you adjust the plan as life circumstances change. Almost all of the successful breakfast transition stories we've heard involve having at least one "trusted advisor" and several surprises— unexpected events both good and bad—along the way.

A word of warning: be very careful in picking an advisor. This must be a person in whom you place the highest degree of personal and professional trust. The decisions you will make in transition could affect you, your family, and those connected to your business for decades.

So dig into this collection of experiences and stories of owners in transition. Skip forward to the topic or step that most speaks to your interests today. Enter this wonderful journey of discovery and abundance. The best is yet to come!

✳ ✳ ✳

1

Uncovering Your Ownership Story: It's Important!

The privilege of a lifetime is being who you are.

Joseph Campbell

If you are an owner who is thinking about selling or passing on your business to the next generation or who is entering a new chapter of life, this book is written specifically for you.

Over nine years of sponsoring confidential breakfasts and listening to "lifetimes" of conversations among business owners and their trusted advisors, we have been most inspired when owners stand in front of a group of their peers and simply tell their real stories.

These breakfast exchanges with owners have convinced us that the very idea of business ownership is significantly different from just owning things. Owners have told us that owning a business requires an "all-in" personal commitment, more so than any other form of ownership in their lives. Over the years, we have heard stories about business leadership, risk taking, motivation, failure, accountability, fairness, long-term and short-term thinking, and the emotional passion owners have for their companies.

When you think about it, a business owner needs to delegate, negotiate, be an example, understand complex rules and regulations, manage finances, and be a responsible community member (among many other tasks) every day of the week. Even in their time off, most owners confess to having difficulty not thinking about their business.

> **Understanding the tenacious grasp that business ownership has on your life can help you move forward in your transition.**

Understanding the tenacious grasp that business ownership has on the life of an owner can help you gain traction to move forward and make a smoother and more meaningful transition.

Owners tell us about personal time and sacrifices they have invested in the business and about the physical and emotional energy they have exerted over the years. It's easy to see why the "owner attachment" is so strong and why the owner-entrepreneur can be so reluctant to "move on." On the flip side, many are so burned out that they long for escape from a self-constructed prison.

During the interactive dialogue in our monthly breakfasts, many owners said they initially felt little urgency when it came to getting started on transition planning: "When things are going well, why rock the boat thinking about leaving the business?"

Many factors create urgency in one's transition decision making. One of our owner-presenters experienced the whack of a big uncontrollable life event: the death of a close friend. When he was confronted by how fragile life is and how "life happens," he said that at least he was in control of his own destiny instead of letting destiny determine his fate. He expressed how important leaving his business would be and how he now felt a personal urgency to start planning. "In all other aspects of my company," he told the group, "I wanted to control as much as humanly possible. Why would I want to do anything less when it comes to a major life decision like passing on my company to a new owner?"

That need for getting started as early as possible was also supported by other successful transition owners, who said it took between five and seven years for their own transitions. And many commented on the unexpected ups and downs that came even with careful planning. "Flexibility in timing and next steps" were words we heard over and over, and they almost always accompanied a successful transition.

There hasn't been a single breakfast over the past nine years where the owner who presented his or her story didn't receive positive feedback on how valuable it was to the other owners and advisors in the audience. So we urge you, as an owner, to think about your story and to realize how special it really is. Then we ask you to think about what it would be like to speak to a private and confidential breakfast audience, with an hour to share important business and life lessons learned with your owner peers. What do you think they would ask you, and how would you answer them? How would your real story unfold?

All of our breakfast speakers have talked about how important it was for them to pull their own stories together and share them with their peers. They said this cathartic exercise helped them realize how personal their businesses and stories were! What is your business transition story? Or, if still afar, your transition dream?

Without a vision, there is no satisfying future.

An old proverb says this, and so do many owners. And the research confirms that no one but you is responsible for initiating and then charting a successful transition path. How do you do this? And most importantly, how do you get started?

Author Annette Simmons, identifies some categories that you can use to tell your business stories:

"Who Am I Stories" can help build your credibility and trust.

"Why Am I Here Stories" can help you explain you journey and even the most frustrating situations.

"Teaching Stories" can help you present the lessons you have learned.

"Vision Stories" can help you explain your ideas for the future of your company.

"Value to Action Stories" helps you to explain your core values and how they affect how you do business.

From *Whoever Tells the Best Story Wins: How to Use Your Own Stories to Communicate with Power and Impact* by Annette Simmons. © 2007 Annette Simmons. Published by AMACOM Books. www.amacombooks.org.

Do you have a future company vision?

Many owners said that the first step to getting serious about a transition was developing a long-range (five to ten years) vision for their companies, for themselves, and for their business partners or families. In truth, in order to get a next-generation owner interested in becoming a successor, a compelling and exciting future for the company needed to be portrayed.

They asked themselves many questions as they developed their long-term company visions: How might the company grow? Could it become a leader in its market? Was there a future strategy for acquisition, or consolidation in a maturing market, for more efficient production, or better quality control via new equipment or improved processes? How about sales and marketing or applying new technology? The owners said they needed to anticipate what a potential new owner or owners would find attractive, compelling, and valuable.

Do you have a personal vision for your future?

Besides advising other owners to think about the future of their companies, many owners also suggested thinking seriously about what to do with life after running a company. One owner stated that the motivation to do better future-life planning was the result of flunking retirement. He said,

"If you don't have a better place calling to you, then you can't leave where you are now."

We also heard story after story about owners wanting to start a new business, solve another problem, spend more time with family and grandchildren, give back to their communities, or travel with their spouses and simply live a less scheduled life after stepping away from their companies.

Having this personal vision of the future is a very important first step in one's transition. If you have passions and interests beyond your company, it will be easier for you to break the strong attachments to your business. This personal vision (which you will see demonstrated throughout this book through owner stories) should also contribute to the urgency of beginning the transition planning process as soon as you are willing to invest time, energy, and money while life is calm. The sooner you begin transition, the sooner you can begin the rest of your life. And the sooner you start, the smarter you will look.

You have a story

- What is the title of your story?

- How much has your story changed from five years ago?

- What do you expect your story to be five years from now?

Are you a clear communicator?

A third universal message we heard from insightful business owners was the need for clear, consistent communication between the owner and family (particularly in family-held businesses), partners, stakeholders, possible successors, and employees.

Every owner knows and has experienced poor communication in the workplace. A missed phone call might result in a misplaced order, and bad instructions on a project will always affect the bottom line because of do-overs. Many owners confessed to not always applying the same rigorous business standards to clearly communicating their transitions at work. Owners who have gone successfully down the path of transition, however, told us that a frequently communicated vision, driven by an attractive path into the future, builds inspiration for employee productivity that is not dependent on the owner/founder. And this means a more valuable business for the owner and the next generation.

The evidence of decades of experience confirms a need for good communication. In their research-based book *Preparing Heirs*, Williams and Preisser report that seven out of ten business transitions fail to reach the next generation for two basic reasons:

1. **Lack of communication.**

2. **Absence of a transition plan with specific steps and timing.**

We know that most small companies do not have regular ownership meetings, keep detailed meeting records, or have a governance structure that requires disciplined internal business communication. This means that an extraordinary effort needs to be made when it comes to developing and communicating your transition plans. Here is a simple formula from our owner experts: involve your own family first, and then involve your business family immediately after you begin your transition.

We believe you will be impressed with the efforts many of our owners made to effectively communicate. Some used "family councils," and others brought in advisors to help articulate plans at company meetings. Some of the owners you

Various methods may be used to effectively communicate your plans as you begin your transition.

will meet took a "business owner's sabbatical." This meant unplugging and stepping away from their businesses long enough to experience unhampered what they had never yet had time to learn, pursue, or explore. This sabbatical time always led to new realizations about what beckoned them into the next stage of life. Often owners used some of the sabbatical to develop a clearer map for themselves and a communication plan for their families, employees, and community.

One owner paused for a sabbatical at his twentieth anniversary in business, saying, "I've been successful, but I don't want the next twenty years to be a repeat of the past twenty years." He came back to the company with a journal showing thirty-seven things he wanted to do in the next stage of life. His leadership team was invited to help him sort through this list, and they selected five things—three for the business and two personal priorities—that are now the focus of his considerable leadership skills, while the energized management team continues in their expanded capacities. His transition plan is very clear and compelling.

Three important rules

These three truths become clear:

1. Find courage to personally tell your business story.

2. Develop a vision of the future for yourself and your company.

3. Be a clear communicator of the future.

These are the first three foundational steps for a successful business and personal transition. Now it's time you meet more visionary owners and hear their stories. We feel confident everyone reading this book will identify with many of the situations that our owners' stories bring to life.

✳ ✳ ✳

2

Finding a Successor: The Next Generation of Ownership

*Life is a succession of crises and opportunities
when we have to rediscover who we are and
what we really want.*

Jean Vanier

A Family-Owned Business Succession Scenario

A few years ago we invited Jenny (not her real name) to tell her transition story at our monthly breakfast gathering. Jenny had been trying to transition from her twenty-five-year business for a long time. We believe the ups and downs of her experience will speak to many thinking about, or even beginning, their own transitions.

Jenny started with a passion for teaching children and an even stronger desire to improve early childhood education in her community. She wanted to respond to the problems many parents face when trying to secure quality, economical, early childhood day care. Jenny had a supportive family, consisting of a husband with his own successful management career and three professional adult children. With their encouragement, she began pursuing her vision.

Jenny told the breakfast audience how the business really "took off" and grew from one small teaching center in a local church to multiple facilities serving 250 children and a professional staff of 30 teachers and aides. Her daughter helped her during this growth phase. This daughter showed both the ability to run the business and some interest in doing so, or in possibly being the next owner. But in many family-owned businesses, things can quickly change.

The change became more evident when Jenny called a family meeting with all children and spouses present. Jenny wanted to clarify who might succeed her when she was ready to leave the business. Her husband was nearing retirement, and even with her passion for the mission of her business, she knew her days as CEO were limited.

When Jenny suggested to the family that in order to have a successful retirement, she needed to sell the business to one of her family members or a group of them, Jenny's children were "blown away." The reality of needing to make a personal investment and take a financial risk in order to own the preschool business was something the children were not ready to do. If fact, Jenny told the breakfast group, this possibility had not really occurred to the children.

Working in the business may be very different from owning the business. Working "in the business" was very different from "owning the business" to the three children. And there was also an unspoken sense of entitlement—meaning they thought the business would simply be passed on to them! Needless to say, Jenny and her husband were surprised in how their children reacted, given the support they had shown working with Jenny and building a successful company.

Shortly after the family meeting, Jenny's daughter moved out of the country to follow her husband in his career. The oldest son, in another state, said he was not interested in owning or running the business, but supported the family doing that. The youngest son was a part-time manager in the family business but left to work full time for a company that offered him an equity ownership. In different ways, the children let Jenny clearly see the evidence that they were not committed and passionate about owning and running the family business.

Let's stop for a moment and look at what might have helped Jenny and her husband better prepare for this transition to a new owner. Almost every business ownership transition we have seen involves passing the torch from one generation to another. We have heard over and over from owners how important it is to have a better understanding of generational differences when they first identify and then negotiate with a successor or new owner—family or not.

Jenny's children are part of the Gen X / Diversity generation. This generation seems reluctant to take the same risks their parents did, especially when it comes to financial investments. We have seen this, curiously enough, even when the children were raised by business entrepreneurs.

They are frequently called the "free agent" generation. They know they have skills—especially those who are involved in private-sector businesses—and they want the freedom to take their skills to the highest bidder, even if it involves putting family loyalties second.

They often do not like to be encumbered with the diverse responsibilities of ownership, and it is not until somewhat later in life that many of them seem ready to assume the role of leading a company or organization. They are very cautious about taking personal financial risks, and they need to carefully "walk through" any risk-taking deal.

Knowing these generational characteristics might have helped Jenny better prepare her children for a future role in the business. She might have explained the "selling process" she envisioned and then helped diminish their fears of a future investment in the company. At the very least, however, these lessons were ones she could apply to a new owner(s) coming from outside of the family.

Jenny outlined for the other owners in the breakfast group the dilemma she now faced with her children no longer in the picture. She wanted to transition away from daily management and ownership, but she couldn't do that unless she felt absolutely sure the new owner would have the same values she brought to this small company. She also wanted to be sure a new owner had the same passion and commitment to the children and parents, which had become a core strength of her brand and reputation.

The good news was that Jenny had nurtured a very talented child-development team over the years. One member of that team was a lead teacher with natural management abilities who supervised one of Jenny's facilities. This lead teacher (whom we shall call Barbara) turned out to have more ambition and a larger vision for the company than just remaining a lead teacher.

Jenny took time with Barbara to explain what she needed to retire and what Barbara would need to do to become the company's new leader. And then Jenny proposed an unusual challenge to Barbara.

Jenny would take a six-month "sabbatical" from the company (with help in planning this from her husband and three children). Barbara would move from lead teacher to interim CEO. She would be responsible for operations during two business quarters, and Jenny promised to not interfere but still be informed of any major business decisions Barbara might make. Jenny called it a "transition sabbatical," and this allowed both her and Barbara to truly experience their new roles.

Jenny went with her husband to the family winter home in Arizona, and Barbara put on her CEO shoes. Both parties found this time extremely valuable and confirming of their beliefs that they were making the right decision. Jenny used some of her "free time" to chart out options and timing for leaving the company, and Barbara was able to chart a vision for the future of the company, which helped alleviate many of the fears she had about taking on the leadership of a long-established company. Jenny would have a role as trusted advisor under Barbara's leadership, and this clarified the path forward in the transition for Jenny. As the transition advanced, Jenny realized she and Barbara needed some outside financial advice to make the ownership bridge as smooth as possible.

A "transition sabbatical" is a valuable tool for learning how to adjust to new roles as the company transitions toward a new generation of leadership.

Since Jenny first decided it was time to move into the next stage of her life, the total time of transition was over eight years. But now the company was finally moving toward a new generation of leadership.

———

According to the National Federation of Independent Businesses (NFIB.com) here are six tips for finding a successor for your company:

1. **Consider family.** If there is someone in your family who you'd like to take over your business, have a conversation with them early on to make sure it's something they even want to do.

2. **Create an evaluation strategy.** If you don't know who would be the best person to take over, come up with a list of criteria that will help you make that choice. You want your business to succeed even after you're gone so this evaluation period will be one of the most important personnel decisions you've ever made.

3. **Consult with top clients.** While you don't have to tell your clients that you're working on a succession plan, you can ask them how they feel about various employees in your organization.

4. **Find out top candidates' intentions.** Talk to your top contenders to find out whether they are committed to your company for the long haul.

5. **Update the successor regarding your plans.** Once you've made your choice, let that person know exactly what you have in mind. That gives that person a chance to develop a sense of ownership in the company and ensures that he or she doesn't look for better opportunities elsewhere.

6. **Announce a succession timeframe.** So that everyone in the organization is on the same page, announce the plans for succession prior to the time that you're actually ready to retire.

A Privately-Held Business Succession Scenario

Another "life-of-its-own" transition story begins with a well-regarded, healthy, professional services firm that had been in business for over fifty years. Founded by three individuals whose names were on the door, it was not family owned.

Two of the three founders were able to exit the business using a well-structured buy-sell agreement with an annually updated valuation of the company and a reasonable time for planned exit. These retirements were funded through operating cash flow of the company, and there was no new debt required. The remaining founder and three younger partners continued leading and owning the business.

The remaining founding partner, in his seventies, and the next most senior partner, in his late sixties, announced their plans to retire in the next two years. This left the two remaining younger partners feeling overwhelmed and unprepared. They said, "We can't do this by ourselves. We need help to keep the company healthy and stay on top of the current workload." The two younger owners carried marketing portfolios, were committed to business development, and were deeply involved in operations. Add to all of this the fact that the company was changing direction—expanding beyond new construction to include renovation and special services—in the aftermath of the 2008 recession, affecting work flow and available cash. There had also been some staff reductions and a reduced investment in infrastructure at this time.

The whole question of the next generation of leadership became a paramount issue for the survival of this company.

When the newer partner came to our breakfast round table discussion, he shared the transition strategy the ownership group had ultimately employed.

He said the four partners decided to try to match the direction they were taking as a company with the core values of a Gen X / Diversity pool of potential leaders in their company. Fifteen engineers/managers were invited to participate in a voluntary leadership-development program that might propel several of them into ownership or top-level management positions. This program required greater responsibility for new business development and mentorship with existing leaders. The goal was developing and demonstrating senior leadership capabilities. The group also set about examining what it might take to help the company improve performance from an operational as well as strategic business-development position.

After three years, two leaders clearly stood out from this group of fifteen. They became "associate principals" with increased compensation and management voting privileges. Senior leadership felt these emerging leaders were on track and hoped they had the confidence to become lead managers for the next generation.

———

In both of these breakfast stories, generational differences played a key role in the transition and succession process. We strongly believe having a mutually clear understanding of all the generations involved in a business sale or leadership/ownership transition can help smooth and speed up the process by minimizing big detours along the journey. It will certainly save you considerable time and money as a business owner.

So here are "Seven Key Lessons" that owners and others have shared with us on succession and generational differences.

Seven Key Lessons

1. Establish criteria for a successor derived from your knowledge of what is required to have the business succeed through a transition in leadership.

You know what has made your business succeed. Make a short list of the skills that have contributed to your success. These skills must be present in the candidates for leading your business forward. However, you should remember that while your and your possible successor's skill sets may be similar or even the same, the same skill set can be expressed in very different ways, particularly in a younger generation. We'll talk more about this later.

2. For a family-owned company, use a "family council" process, mentioned above in passing but not elaborated upon, to communicate succession needs and opportunities for family members.

Consider defining and publishing the requirements for a family member to be considered an employee, manager, or leader of the family business. Invite all family members who meet the requirements to be potential candidates. Review and evaluate all family candidates, and communicate the results of your review. Clear, open communication on a consistent basis is essential.

3. Assess capabilities and interests of one or more successor candidates.

Use professional resources, such as an industrial psychologist, to perform the assessments. Apply assessment findings to personalized development plans for successors. We strongly recommend a succession plan that uses an external resource experienced in profiling and assessing the fit of candidates for an important business leadership role. Identified strengths and weaknesses of candidates will then be further developed in time, and gaps may be covered by other managers.

4. Select potential successors who you are confident can effectively run your business.

Our experience shows that it takes multiple candidates to reach the end of a five-year development plan, with at least one candidate on track. Owners need a backup plan and other potential candidates in the event that "life" intervenes and the preferred successor isn't available at the desired transition time. Conduct annual leadership-development progress reviews with your potential successor or successors. Reward exemplary performance in any expanded roles with increased compensation based on financial performance each year. Update your succession plan each year.

5. Prepare a written succession development plan.

Show realistic time lines looking out five or more years. It's essential to start with more than one candidate. Report annual progress and make changes to the plan as appropriate. Start your transition plans with clear role definitions for key managers and succession candidates. As your transition plan unfolds year to year, your role as owner/leader must diminish as the impact of successors increases. Map out what you do now, and also show what other key managers do. Indicate how you will gradually transfer responsibilities from you to them in each year going forward.

6. **If you don't have a clear successor, or a likely successor steps out of the picture, develop alternative plans to address this need.**

Consider turning to a qualified internal candidate who is not a family member. Consider an interim, nonfamily manager to lead the business during the development and mentoring time required for a family successor to grow into the position.

7. **Consider selling the business as a viable alternative.**

Set a future time to decide whether you have the right candidates to succeed you. If the confidence isn't there (after two or three years at the most), shift to another candidate or move on to another option that may include selling the business

Three questions to ponder on succession:

1. Who other than yourself can run your business?

2. How ready are you to turn over control to a younger manager?

3. How confident are you in the leadership of your highest potential successor?

✳ ✳ ✳

3

Understanding the Next Generation

Each generation imagines itself to be more intelligent than the one that went before it, and wiser than the one that comes after it.

George Orwell

The reason people blame things on previous generations is that there's only one other choice!

Doug Larson

The topic of how to understand the next generation of leadership was most in demand for our breakfast round tables. So we want to give you a short introduction in understanding who you are from a generational perspective.

Owners talked about the differences between themselves, their children, and nonrelated younger leaders in their companies. The many concerns raised by senior business leaders included: "I don't understand their work ethic." "What is all this social media about?" "Don't people just meet in person anymore and figure out how to solve problems?"

Younger potential successors at the breakfast would often ask: "Why does it take so long to get things done here?" "What is all of this process stuff about?" "Why should I be asked take a big risk with my career?" "What specific skills will I take with me if I have to leave this company?"

A father who was trying to pass his business on to his son described the generational differences in this way: "For my son, the business experience seemed like a sprint; for me, it was always a marathon experience."

We recommend that our owners and potential owners first try to better understand their own generations and how they acquired their core values and particular business work styles.

The members of every generation acquire their "core values" at a very young age (between ten and fifteen years of age), and these core values stay with them for the rest of their lives. The core values often emerge strongly in a time of crisis or during major transitions.

Accumulated values become secondary to core values in a time of crisis or transition. Each generation also acquires and accumulates values as its members grow into adulthood. And while the accumulated values—such as what you own or your professional titles and honors—are important, they become secondary to core values in a time of crisis or transition. Core values—like family, relationships, honesty, integrity, faith, and love—are so deep within us that we often take them for granted. However, when we are in the midst of a crisis and looking for some solid ground to stand on, our core values come to the surface and help us move forward on our journey. (Chapter 5 helps you identify your core values.)

If you were born between 1940 and 1963 and have owned a business for a number of years, you hold business values in common with other people from your generation. You share:

- a strong work ethic

- integrity

- loyalty

- determination

- commitment to your product or service

- seeing your work and family as interrelated and equally important.

In addition:

- You are educated—either formally or through your business experiences and training. You understand that the best way to deal with change is by trying to be prepared for it. And if there are bumps along the way, you have something saved for the rough times.

- Some might describe you as a seasoned business professional. The hours you spend at work are not considered as important as providing the best product or service for your clients or customers. For you, the customer is the first priority, and quality follows close behind. You are careful about taking risks, getting into debt, and increasing your bottom line. You enjoy the satisfaction of doing a good job, making your customer happy, and making a little profit in the process.

- Your "business promises" have meant something, and your identity is closely tied to your business. You have been "hands-on" in your company, and you probably personally know most of your major customers or clients.

- **You understand the concept of "delayed gratification" and know that by working hard and saving, you will be able to more fully enjoy the fruits of your labor at a later date and have something to pass on to your family.**

It is most likely that your business successor will come from a completely different generation. He or she will probably be a member of the Gen X / Diversity generation (born between 1964 and 1984 and now between thirty and fifty years old). This is a generation born into the era of "free agency." Its members firmly believe that if they have a proven business skill set, they can sell themselves to the highest bidder. Many do not see themselves initially as owners, and this is an important transition issue for you to deal with first.

This generation often puts family and friends ahead of work and business. They are the "day care" and "divorced parents" generation. They often spent a good deal of time alone as children and relied on their peers for social and emotional support. It is not surprising that many of these younger managers are willing to sacrifice financial rewards for the sake of maintaining their family and friend relationships. This is the generation that has fueled the homeschooling movement.

We know that 80 percent of the privately held small and midsize businesses in this country will be involved in a business transition in the next twenty years. In Minnesota alone, over 18,000 businesses went through a transition in 2014.

And the Fox Small Business Center reports that sales of small businesses grew 49 percent in 2013, according to a new report by business-for-sale marketplace BizBuySell.

Members of the Gen X / Diversity generation try to differentiate between having a strong work ethic and "workaholism." Many have seen their parents be workaholics, and the results have not been particularly good for them. They do not have the same sense of loyalty that you have to an employer. With ownership, this can change, but it is important to understand where your successor may be on the loyalty continuum.

This generation's members see many relationships as short term, and they prize options. While you may see your business as a marathon, they may see it as a sprint. You can help change their construct to seeing the future of your business as a "series of sprints." They love technology and believe in "high tech, high touch." This can be a real benefit for the future, given our society's acceptance of technology as a primary business delivery platform. You will need to understand the importance of social networking, short but clearly defined business meetings, and a different accountability model that relies more on results than on how the results were achieved.

When it comes to financing an ownership transition, you and your trusted advisor might meet your greatest challenge. This younger generation is often not willing to invest its own money in business opportunities. Its members are not opposed to financing if they are in the business, but many do not trust bankers and complicated financial deals. We recommend that you find someone closer in age to your successor to help develop your deal. This will help establish a common language and increase the trust level. The simpler the deal, the better, and the more you can show a successor that ownership involves a personal financial risk, the easier your deal conversation will be.

We hope these tips will help you pick a good successor and assist you in your transition.

Three questions to consider

1. What generation does your successor belong to?

2. How comfortable are you with the differences between his or her generation and yours?

3. What ongoing communication are you using with the next generation to understand and accommodate these differences?

Now look at your business more closely and at what you need to do to make it easier to understand. Then try and translate your business passion into making your company more attractive to the next generation of ownership.

✳ ✳ ✳

4

Getting Your Business Ready for Transition

The price of success is hard work, dedication to the job at hand, and the determination that whether we win or lose, we have applied the best of ourselves to the task at hand.

Vince Lombardi

Getting your business ready for sale or for a transition is somewhat like selling a home, but it's a lot more complicated. The business needs to have "curb appeal" (be attractive to a successor), and it needs to pass a rigorous inspection process ("due diligence" conducted by a potential buyer) before any sale. But that's where the comparisons stop.

There is a huge interest today in "flipping houses." When you flip a home, you usually make cosmetic changes to try to increase its value, like new paint, new appliances, knocking down a wall to make more space, etc. You can't make these kinds of changes to your company and expect good results. Quite the contrary, cosmetic changes will quickly appear as such with the potential buyers' due diligence, making your business overall much less attractive.

In our years of working with business owners, we have heard of some extremely creative and substantive changes owners have made to make their businesses ready for sale or transition to a family member. There are no rigid rules for getting your business ready for your personal transition; there are only sound and validated best practices by business owners in comparable markets.

We would like to share two of our favorite breakfast stories and provide you with a short checklist of what you need to think about when you are ready to take that next big step in your life. Here are two owners who were willing to share this part of their journey with you.

Taking a Creative Approach to a Transition

It was a warm summer morning when Phil stood up before our breakfast gathering and said matter-of-factly that if he had wanted to, he could have closed up shop, sold his equipment and furniture, liquidated other assets, and lived a very comfortable life in retirement. "But," he quickly continued, "that would not have been fair to my employees and their families, our longtime customers, and the community where we had been located for over twenty years and contributed a significant amount of economic impact." That revenue, he said, helped to pay for education and needed services in the community in which he lived and worked.

Phil told the breakfast audience that he had come up with a different vision to make his transition plans more meaningful for everyone connected to his company.

Phil contacted a trusted advisor with his somewhat irregular but intriguing idea. There was a well-respected competitor that served the same market. The company was roughly the same size as Phil's, had about the same number of employees, and was geographically not far from where Phil's plant was located.

"What do you think about merging the two companies?" Phil asked his trusted advisor, Jack. After the merger, Phil would stay on through the birth of the new and larger company and then allow the new company to buy out his interests.

Jack had done a number of interesting deals in his life, but this one was unique among all the transition strategies he had encountered. Phil wanted to be sure the merger would keep as many current employees from both firms as possible (a reflection of his business ethics) and continue the corporate culture both companies practiced in common. He also wanted to improve the likelihood of a sustained transition by raising the value of the new and larger company.

Raising the value of the company in transition can create a beneficial situation for both the owner in transition and the future of the company.

Jack suggested that if the other company were interested, he should be retained separately by both companies to fairly represent both of their interests. The other company was excited about the deal and secured Jack to also represent them, and the merger process began.

Phil told his breakfast peers that in a short time a stand-alone evaluation was completed, and both parties came to a basic agreement on the overall shape of the merger. It turned out that Phil's company was worth a little more than his merger partner's, so a cash payment was made to Phil to even up the difference. No employees were let go as a result of the merger!

The one stumbling block for both companies was their respective inventories. Both companies thought the other's inventory was overvalued and should not be counted in the final financial tally. Phil said that Jack proposed a fair and equitable solution. Their mutual advisor suggested that both companies write off a certain part of their respective inventories and use the write-off as a tax benefit before the merger. Phil told the group, "That was the benefit of using consulting help when it comes to major business deals."

After two years of helping move the new and larger company into a stronger profit condition by leading new business development, Phil was bought out by his new partners. He concluded his breakfast talk by saying that he was entering a new phase of life more relaxed, enjoying his family, and trying out new things with the extra time he didn't expect to have.

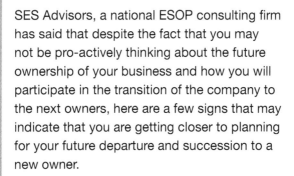

SES Advisors, a national ESOP consulting firm has said that despite the fact that you may not be pro-actively thinking about the future ownership of your business and how you will participate in the transition of the company to the next owners, here are a few signs that may indicate that you are getting closer to planning for your future departure and succession to a new owner.

1. I'd like to be ready to sell if the opportunity presents itself.

2. No one else can run this business except for me and I'm uncomfortable with that fact.

3. My friends are getting sick and I want to relax and enjoy life before I do too.

4. I made my contribution to this business and my kids don't want it.

Life and Cheaper Competition Happens!

One of the more complex transition stories we have heard in recent years involved a family-owned, second-generation, custom-manufacturing company.

This company was struggling after business had plateaued following years of growth and had then become unprofitable due to cut-throat pricing from lower-cost competition. The

Family business is difficult, challenging, and rewarding.

husband and wife owners, George and Delores, had two sons who left other firms to join the family business. The sons were committed to developing stronger operational performance, improving sales growth, and instituting better cost controls in their family company.

George and Delores wanted to transition out of the business and pass it on to their sons. But they knew they first needed to restructure the manufacturing operation, define a new customer base, establish some strong financial reporting procedures, and even develop new proprietary products if possible. They hired a consultant to help the family and the business move forward.

When the consultant, whom we will call Jim, showed them that the new manufacturing skills could be adapted to their existing manufacturing capabilities, they were off and running.

With the whole family and the consultant working together, they improved manufacturing procedures, trained production employees, reduced work in process, set up new quality control steps, pruned their current customer list and eliminated unprofitable customers. New proprietary products began to show promise, and their quality performance and reputation was restored. Now the question of the owners transitioning returned to the top of the owners' priority list.

As owners and parents, they knew it was time for them to pull away, but first they had some hard decisions to make about the performance and leadership structure of their business.

Define and use policies that guide the employment of family members.
They knew their sons were fully prepared to manage profit and loss responsibilities. Even though there was some push-back on this issue from the sons' point of view, the owners decided to hire an interim president for a five-year transition. While the sons were not completely happy with that decision, they trusted their parents' promise that the sons would run the business and the parents would respect their boundaries. Both sons had significant management responsibilities under the new business organization.

Then, as in many family-owned companies, earlier family issues emerged. George still wanted to stay actively involved in sales and new business development while his sons provided operational leadership and support of the new interim president. The sons wanted their father and mother to exit from active management in the core business so they could interact directly with the interim president. Jim, the consultant, suggested they hold a "family council" that he would facilitate.

Jim's help was timely. It helped them agree on a solution that nobody had anticipated. The family acquired a small proprietary manufacturing company that used a complementary manufacturing process for a unique line of products with established customers and distribution channels. This action took George and Delores out of the core business but kept them "tangentially" involved because the core business now supplied products for the newly acquired business.

By implementing the family council, the owners and next generation were able to define roles that were both challenging and distinct that did not overlap with one another. They set boundaries for both companies, and George and Delores focused on running the new smaller business. Parents, when out of the business, have a different relationship with their children. The two boys entered a formal ownership transfer agreement wherein their parents' retirement would be funded over a twenty-year period with distributions from the original company that the boys were now leading.

Planning, open communication, and a family council with outside advisors is valuable during the transition process.

"All in all," George said, "the organization of the business was fair and met everybody's needs." Delores added, "This would not have happened unless there was clear and honest communication among all the family members that led to clarity of roles and responsibilities. It was very important that we were able to address and agree on key points."

———

Here is a summary of what we have we learned from our breakfast presenters Phil, George, and Delores (along with other owners) about getting your business ready to sell or transfer:

1. **Be creative.** There is almost always a solution for positioning your business for a transition—if you are flexible and open to new ideas.

2. **Use professional help when you are stuck or can't seem to get started.** A trusted advisor can save you time, money, and a lot of aggravation in a transition scenario related to the organization and presentation of your company.

3. **Be clear and honest about how YOU want the company to look and what your "bottom lines" are** for lifestyle, ongoing activities of the owner, and financial needs.

4. **Get an objective professional valuation of your business**, including your intellectual property.

5. **Talk to a tax advisor** and get his or her opinion on the best corporate ownership structure for a sale or family transfer with the most favorable tax consequences.

6. **Be prepared to answer key due-diligence questions.** The best way to do that is to ask those questions of yourself as a potential buyer and then prepare good answers. This always means having updated corporate documents.

A sequence of steps in expected transition events was squarely addressed by our next breakfast storytellers. They spoke with intensity about the importance of having a personal and business transition plan—and being willing to listen.

✳ ✳ ✳

5

Designing a Personal and Business Transition Plan

Live out your imagination, not your history.

Steven Covey

Imagine you have it all—a successful company you run with your spouse, adequate savings, a daughter who is interested in taking over the company, and plenty of interests to pursue when your business career comes to an end. And then the unexpected life event occurs.

A serious illness changed everything for Hank and his wife. And to make matters worse, his daughter and two senior managers found there wasn't enough money in current cash flow to buy the company from Hank and his wife so they could begin the retirement they'd imagined. Hank stood before the breakfast group, with his daughter in the audience, and shared this very personal and at times moving succession scenario.

Hank and his wife realized they had not done the kind of financial planning that could have made for the simple succession of their daughter and two other potential partners. When their cash flow leveled off during the 2008 recession, they were able to stay stable but did not have enough cash for an immediate buyout.

Their personal financial planning did not account for the expenses that resulted from Hank's unexpected illness.

The business was able to hold its own, so he and his wife would need to find a different financial solution for their difficult situation. Hank went to his accountant and asked him what he would recommend to facilitate a buyout from the business as quickly as possible.

After a careful study of the company and Hank's personal finances, the CPA firm helped build a detailed five-year performance model. This showed that available cash flow from sustained operating margins with modest revenue growth (if managed as well as revenue had historically been managed) could provide funding for the purchase of founder's equity during the five-year window. This was not exactly what Hank wanted to hear, but it was a sound plan.

Upon reflection, this time period would allow Hank and his wife to gradually transition to more time up north at their lake home. It would also allow his daughter and two senior managers to put in place the CPA firm's managed growth strategies. Finally, the five-year plan offered performance-based incentives paid to the succession team with vesting provisions and other performance requirements. At the completion of the five-year plan, the succession team would purchase controlling interest from Hank and his wife, with voting control staying in family hands.

At the completion of a second five-year period, Hank's accountants felt the succession team would have accumulated sufficient performance-based incentive funds to acquire the remaining shares from the founder and voting control for themselves.

Hank told the group that having this kind of long-term business plan in place enabled him and his wife to focus independently on their personal and financial plans for the next ten years. He said, "I wish I had thought about this five years earlier!"

In a question-and-answer session following the presentation, Hank stressed to the other owners the importance of good financial planning and making sure to consider the unexpected events that happen during our lives. Hank said, "You never know when life can change, and it can change in an instant. I was fortunate to have a strong business, a supportive family, and great advisors to help me get through a difficult time. I can tell you, I wasn't able to think clearly when I felt I was under pressure. Fortunately, I was willing to listen."

> **You never know when life can change, and it can change in an instant.**

Make Me an Offer!

Another owner began his breakfast presentation in this way: "Our boutique manufacturing business and our industry took a major hit after 9/11, and I wasn't sure where I saw myself in the future. I wanted the company to recover but was unsure if I had the energy or the passion to build it back up. My independent streak had hit a real roadblock. I needed some professional help and some peer guidance." Lou, our owner and presenter, did not have a business or personal financial plan that covered his situation, and he knew it.

Lou explained to the group that his initial mistake was not recognizing the importance of having a plan allowing for contingencies like 9/11. In retrospect he told the breakfast gathering, "I did not know how to incorporate personal transition issues driven by the demands of the business into our family without sending a message of entitlement or expectation. It was important to me that both my sons had freedom to find their own careers, passions, and independence. Because both of my sons had developed highly successful and financially rewarding careers with multinational corporations, I assumed that neither would want to come into the business, which effectively cut off the possibility of a 'family succession plan.' Too bad I never asked!"

When developing your transitional business and personal financial plans—especially if you are a smaller family business—you should not assume you know what your children think about the business or how they might want to participate in your transition from it. You have to ask. You can engage family members in a direct conversation, or you can have an outsider conduct interviews with all members of the family.

In the fall of 2002, Lou started having serious concerns about what to do with his boutique manufacturing business—sell it or work until age ninety. He was having lunch with his son Doug, then thirty-four. Doug had recently been named US salesman of the year at his company (among a sales force of 1,100) and was considering new opportunities. When they met to talk over Doug's résumé, Lou remembers saying something like, "Son, our business needs a sales manager with your qualifications." His son's unexpected response to his father was, "Make me an offer."

Lou told the breakfast group that he was completely taken aback by Doug considering working in the family business. This lunch was a pivotal moment for him. He was excited but also terrified about bringing Doug into the business. He said, "I wrestled with this emotional conflict and internalized the decision. I didn't discuss it with my wife—a major mistake! I never reached out for help and didn't consider the effect of the decision on our company, its management team, or our family—especially on Doug's younger brother, Thomas. Only much later did I learn that Thomas had always hoped that he would ultimately take over the family business."

We strongly advise that before you decide to bring a family member into the business, you create a family council, even if you don't think you need one yet. A colleague reminded us when we started writing this book that all happy families are happy in the same way, while all unhappy families are unhappy in their own distinct ways!

A family council provides a framework for regular communication to educate the family about business transition, to address and resolve conflicts, and to identify emerging interests in the family enterprise as children and grandchildren grow up. It also offers an open forum to discuss opportunities, qualifications, and desires. The goal is to prevent unintended consequences that will most likely have negative ramifications for other family members. It can also be a way of creating some fun family events.

A good transition plan consists of 5 basic elements:

1. A personal vision of your future beyond the business.
2. A successor development plan.
3. A financing vehicle.
4. A legal buy-sell agreement.
5. A sound evaluation of your business.

A few months after his lunch with Doug, and before the announcement of Doug's new role as national sales manager, Lou came face-to-face with the guardian of his family's relationships: his wife, Cheryl. And he knew immediately that he was in trouble. His other son, Thomas, and his wife were visiting for Christmas on the day that he and Doug reached an agreement. He casually mentioned to Cheryl that he was "thinking" of bringing Doug into the business. She was astonished and quickly asked, "What about Thomas?" She was loud, strong, and clear: "You may be responsible for the company, but don't blow up the family."

Thomas did not take the news well. He was highly qualified. But the reality was that his strengths mirrored his brother's in sales and marketing. Within a small company, there simply wasn't another opportunity for him. Thomas was hurt, disappointed, and angry. Simply put, Thomas was devastated not to have even been asked. Lou sadly shared with the group, "I have very few regrets in my life, but this one tops the list. I could have—and should have—handled this decision so much better. It's a lesson I learned the hard way, and I share the story often with family business owners as a way to help make amends. It is a lesson in the importance of inclusive planning, personally and organizationally."

Lou also discussed the agony he felt over announcing Doug's appointment to his top managers. They had assumed the two sons were not coming into the business. During a managers' meeting, he said he had hired a new national sales manager whom he felt was well qualified for the job. When he passed out Doug's résumé with the name removed, one of the managers said, "Wow! Is this your son Doug?" The general reaction was favorable; however, one individual, who might have been a candidate to take over the position as president, felt threatened and was visibly upset. That individual never adapted to Doug being in the company and left within a year.

Since 2002, Lou's other son, Thomas, has moved into a different industry sector where he has now worked for the past ten years. He is very proud of his success and is well recognized within the company for his accomplishments. Although they live in different states and have very busy professional and family lives, Doug and Thomas have maintained a good relationship, including a shared interest in running marathons.

And while Lou had not taken the time to create a long-range personal and business plan, one of Doug's first steps was to build a long-range growth plan, which the company had never had before. This placed the company on a growth trajectory and enabled Lou to take a sabbatical and really explore his own transition out of the business. Lou told the breakfast group, "While it may seem cheaper to do your own transition and long-term business planning, it is cheaper in the long term to ask for help and develop comprehensive long-term plans. You can't do this alone."

> **While it may seem cheaper to do your own transition and long-term business planning, it is cheaper in the long term to ask for help and develop comprehensive long-term plans. You can't do this alone.**

Doug earned the respect of the company's employees, customers, and suppliers. It was important to the transitioning owner that everyone saw him as the leader in charge. Lou related that when he returned from his five-month sabbatical, he called a company meeting (including local family members) on a Thursday and announced Doug's promotion to president, effective the next day. The short transition period was painless and could not have been more successful. There was no time for staff to speculate or question "who was in charge."

In fact, there was immediate enthusiastic support. The company moved forward and never missed a beat. Doug's long-term strategic plan sent a strong message about the sustainability of the business, and it ensured his position as the person in charge.

Lou now volunteers in public service. He is also exploring other ways to give back to the community. In addition, he still consults with Doug on business issues as needed and attends periodic company meetings—as well as traveling, gardening, reading, and spending time with his five grandchildren. As he puts it, "After a forty-year career, I'm enjoying being an owner without the concerns of daily operations, and I am grateful for the freedom and flexibility I now have to pursue other passions and opportunities."

As you continue to develop and refine your transition goals and objectives, you and your trusted advisor will need to consider long-range financial plans for both your business and personal life, your legacy, retirement funding, next-generation needs if appropriate, and especially charitable-giving interests. Our experience clearly reveals that there is an abundance of assets, both intangible and tangible, that owners may not fully realize they possess and have the capacity to direct in the usual twenty-five years remaining of postmanagement life.

Three questions to ponder

1. How attractive is the five-year outlook for your business?

2. What is the probability of realizing this business performance?

3. What are the highest uncontrollable risks in your business outlook?

Based on Hank's and Lou's stories, we urge you to prepare long-range financial and organizational projections for your business. This will allow you to better assess the feasibility of owning the business during an internal succession process, or possibly prepare you for a sale to a new owner if there is significant doubt about getting paid what you want for your business. Guidance for a keep-or-sell decision is always complicated and depends on many variables, such as long-term family financial interests, availability of qualified candidates, support of family shareholders, availability of capital and debt, and broader economic conditions. Having a financial transition plan helps define your priorities and points to your best options as the years pass.

As you have seen in our two stories, personal and family financial needs must also be clearly defined at important milestones along the transition path. Even though you are trying to make a sound business decision in your transition, it is your passions, your love for your family, and your need to leave a lasting legacy that will not only propel you to act but also sustain you during the transition process.

Your plans should address core financial needs to meet both personal and family lifestyle expectations, funding for next-generation interests, and charitable giving. Basic assumptions on risk, return, inflation, liquidity, and family legacy should be reflected in a long-term plan that will guide your pre- and post-transition decisions. But remember what Lou said: "Never be afraid to consult others, and never be afraid to ask."

The key thing is to act on these plans now when you don't have an urgent need. At least, that is what owners tell us!

✳ ✳ ✳

6

Making Personal Lifestyle Choices: Post-Ownership

We don't see things as they are, we see them as we are.

Anaïs Nin

Franklin carries a very large persona in his life and his business. People often describe him as "larger than life." As the owner of three very successful banks, he had very few concerns other than keeping his business growing.

His handsome looks, authoritative voice, wonderful sense of humor, impeccable clothes, and incredible rags-to-riches story propelled him to natural leadership positions in the Rotary, professional business organizations, his church, and community boards.

When Franklin came to our breakfast, he wanted to talk about what had happened to him just a few years after successfully selling his banks and making enough in the sale that he and his immediate family would never have to worry about money again.

"I thought I had it all," he told the group. "My wife and I both loved golf, our grandchildren, and we loved to travel. We would spend retirement enjoying our lives and never look back. That's what I thought."

Franklin went on to share with the group that after a couple of years of doing what "he really loved," he felt unsatisfied and was having increasing episodes of depression. He lacked the ambition and initiative that had been so natural when he was running his banks, and he started gaining weight. His wife suggested counseling. His friends found him hard to be around. Franklin summed it up for the breakfast gathering quite well when he said, "Look, in a two-year time frame, I literally went from who's who in my community to who's he?" And he reminded the breakfast group what Mark Twain had said: "The worst loneliness is not to be comfortable with yourself."

It took a few years, but Franklin found some new interests to pursue and turned the "second half" of his life around. He spoke at the breakfast because he wanted other owners to know that his journey would have been much less painful for him and his family if he had thought about retirement differently—if he had started planning this phase of his transition much earlier.

Franklin's story is like those of hundreds of other former owners we have met. There is only so much golf you can play or so many trips you can take before you begin to ask yourself, is this all that there is? And while your work might have been demanding and intrusive on your personal time, it provided meaning and varied forms of satisfaction over a very long period.

> **Boomers were the first generation to define their identities primarily through work life.**

Boomers have additional pressures that arise when they transition from their own companies. Unlike many of their parents, who could easily separate work and personal time, boomers were the first generation to define their identities primarily through work life. What they did at work became synonymous with what they defined as a meaningful life.

We have found fewer and fewer boomers thinking about retirement in the traditional sense. They are members of the best educated, most affluent, and most well-traveled generation in history. They're asking very different questions: What do I really want to do in the next phase of my life? What are my passions, and how can I build on them to determine my future? Are there opportunities to continue working, but for fewer hours or in a different capacity? How can I transform my work skills into meaningful volunteer work? Is it too late to start a new career? What about starting another business? And finally, hauntingly, how can I make sure I reach the end of my life knowing that I lived the most meaningful, fulfilling life possible?

The whole concept of retirement—literally meaning that we withdraw from the activities that have taken over 150,000 hours in our lives up to age sixty-five—is difficult for many boomers to understand. That is why every national poll shows that over 85 percent of them do not want to quit working, but instead do different kinds of work and in different ways.

Connecting with Your Core Values First

It is very difficult to chart a path to your future until you better understand your core values and the importance of your hopes and dreams. Exploring core values is a wonderful gift to yourself. In the day-to-day business of our lives, we seldom take time to reflect on the powerful question "Who am I, really?" This is now your chance.

Determining Your Core Values

How many people like Franklin do you know who have good incomes, important jobs, luxury cars, and beautiful homes, but who are not truly happy or satisfied with their lives? The offices of counselors and psychiatrists are filled with people who look as if they have it all. Yet something is missing in their lives. The missing element may simply be confusion, or a lack of clarity about their core values.

Core values are the deep values you learned at a young age, such as:

- **Honesty**
- **Belonging**
- **Respect**
- **Giving something back through service to others**

These basic values tend to get buried by the stuff you accumulate in your life and by things our culture considers important—such as job titles, automobiles, club memberships, and material possessions. Whether you like it or not, the question of who you truly are only emerges at midlife. You confront events that forever change the way you see yourself. Your children are older and no longer need you in the same way they did. Perhaps someone significant in your life dies, you find out a close friend has cancer, or your career path takes an unexpected turn because of downsizing or a corporate merger. With these life changes, you begin to look much deeper within yourself. When you do, you can find strength in the basic core values with which you grew up.

Honoring your values means living in a way that is congruent with who you really are. Many people experience dissatisfaction and anxiety when they reach a key transition in midlife and realize that they aren't living their values. If there is dissonance between your authentic self (your values) and how you live (your lifestyle), unhappiness inevitably will result. An important part of refiring your life is living in harmony with who you are by honoring your values.

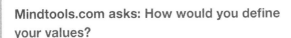

Mindtools.com asks: How would you define your values?

Before you answer this question, you need to know what, in general, values are.

Your values are the things that you believe are important in the way you live and work.

They (should) determine your priorities, and, deep down, they're probably the measures you use to tell if your life is turning out the way you want it to.

When the things that you do and the way you behave match your values, life is usually good—you're satisfied and content. But when these don't align with your values, that's when things feel... wrong. This can be a real source of unhappiness.

This is why making a conscious effort to identify your values is so important. They suggest that you Identify the times when you were happiest,

Identify the times when you were most proud, and then Identify the times when you were most fulfilled and satisfied...

Here are a few activities that will help you identify, clarify, prioritize, and honor your core values by putting them into action:

Exercise 1: Identify Your Values

Who are you deep down inside? What values describe your most authentic self? Make a list of your most important values. If you find this very difficult, think about people you greatly admire. Think about who those people are and what they do that makes them so admirable. Those traits are probably some of your values.

Exercise 2: Clarify Your Values

Clarifying your values involves a simple test. Pick a value that you consider core from your list above. Then ask these questions:

- **How did I acquire this value?**
- **Did I choose it consciously, or did I accept it from somebody else?**
- **Is it something I regularly act upon?**
- **Do I practice this value because I want to?**
- **Do I plan on practicing it for the rest of my life?**
- **If someone challenged this value, would I be willing to explain it in public?**

If you can answer a passionate yes to each one of these questions, that value is true and core to you.

Exercise 3: Prioritize Your Values

From your list above, select the three that are most important in making you who you are. Consider this question: If you were marooned on a desert island with only three of your core values as company, which three would you choose?

Find Your Passion and What Spirits You

After you have identified your core values, you can turn to what gives you passion or spirit. The inner flame that is your spirit can sometimes be brought low by the pace and distractions of modern life. Why do you think it's called "burnout?" You can kindle your spark through awareness of what spirits you. You can reignite the flame by focusing on the people you love, showing gratitude for what brings you joy, and allowing yourself to fulfill your deepest wishes.

Eliza's Story

At the age of sixty, Eliza found herself reflecting on her life. A self-employed professional, she was quite successful in her field. She had two adult children and enjoyed spending time with her grandchildren. After a serious illness, she found herself feeling somewhat empty, as though something were missing in her life. She wondered what her life really meant.

One afternoon when Eliza was spending time with an old friend, she started talking about a writers' workshop she attended every summer. She said, "You know, I just love to write." And as she talked about writing, her whole being lit up. Her face softened and changed. Her hands flew up to her heart, her eyes closed, and she looked peaceful and happy. She was transformed.

Her friend pointed out that Eliza always "blissed out" at the writers' workshop, yet she never tried writing as a serious hobby or profession on her own. Eliza had a standard reply about her clients and the difficulty of getting away from work. Her friend said, "What are you really afraid of?" Eliza said, "I'm afraid I'll end up out on the street with no money and nowhere to go." The two of them started to laugh. Eliza could easily cut back on her hours and workload if she wanted to and still be fine financially, yet she never tried writing.

Her friend said, "You know, you're such a terrific person. Writing makes you so happy. It would be very sad if you died without ever having sung your song."

Each of us has elements in our lives that "spirit" us, that make us feel alive and in the moment. Common activities that spirit us include enjoying nature, humor, being part of a faith community, sports, meditation, being with friends, travel, adventure, pets, hobbies, and music. Unfortunately, the rush of daily life often crowds out activities that nourish us. And sometimes fear gets in the way, especially the fear of trying something new. Often those fears are unrealistic, but nonetheless prevent us from moving ahead.

Finding What Distracts and Dulls You

As the saying goes, even if you win the rat race, you're still a rat! Our spirits are constantly bombarded by media appeals to the materialistic side of our natures. It is difficult to escape electronic and print advertising on TV, the Internet, radio, billboards, flyers, and in magazines and direct mail. While we can turn off the TV and ignore the mail, we're assaulted with video screens in airports, on gas pumps, and in elevator lobbies. There are even ad posters in public restrooms. News media concentrate on bad news, replaying images over and over again, so many people believe that the world is a much more dangerous place than it is. We are constantly provoked by stimuli that enhance unrealistic fears. The sheer volume of exposure to negative images over time is enough to throw our lives out of balance. We call this being "dulled." Your spirit feels dull, and it becomes difficult to find those parts of yourself that respond to a higher calling. Is your spirit asking you to turn off the clutter? Here are some signs:

- **You don't take time to meet your own needs or take care of yourself.**

- **You are always saying, "I'm too busy."**

- **Your consumption of caffeine is getting higher and higher.**

- **You find it very difficult to pray or meditate.**

- **You carry your cell phone on the golf course, at dinner, or to other recreational activities.**

- **You find it very difficult to treat yourself to something special.**

Eliza sat down and thought through just how unrealistic her fears were. Her friend was right—finances and clients were not keeping her from writing. This left her asking whether she really did want to write. She decided to challenge herself. She blocked out some time on her calendar to visit her friend's beach house and vowed that she would write for at least four hours a day. What would she learn about herself? What if she couldn't do it? What if she loved it as much as she thought she might? It was time to find out. Eliza scheduled the trip to the beach house, full of anticipation, excitement, and a fear of the unknown that made her feel giddy and very much alive.

We know that many of you will never be able to begin your transition process unless you discover a more exciting place to go than work. If you base your new journey on your core values, your passions, and nurturing your spirit, your postwork options will be much brighter and certainly more meaningful and sustainable. You will become a better person ready to continue an interesting legacy!

Three questions to ponder

1. What are your financial needs to the end of your expected life?

2. How reliable is your estimate of retirement funding from 401(k)/IRA and business income?

3. What plans do you have for sharing and giving back some of your abundance?

✳ ✳ ✳

7

Defining a Genuine Legacy

It doesn't matter what you do, so long as you change something from the way it was before you touched it into something that's like you after you take your hands away. The difference between the man who just cuts lawns and a real gardener is in the touching. The lawn-cutter might just as well not have been there at all; the gardener will be there a lifetime.

Ray Bradbury, *Fahrenheit 451*

Many owners have told us that having something they considered more important to do with their lives was a strong incentive for making a transition away from being responsible for their companies. A favorite expression was that nobody wanted to die with their "boots on"—meaning they didn't want to die at work. There is a great deal to be learned by simply listening to how owners made the choices they did for the second half of their lives.

We know that a legacy is something you are creating and building your entire life. It doesn't magically appear when you are ready to transition. We also know that as you near your transition moment, your legacy sometimes comes into a much clearer focus.

Here are three questions you can ask yourself when you are thinking about life after work...

1. How would you like to be remembered, or what will be your legacy?

2. Is your legacy more than your business?

3. Are you currently involved with philanthropic or community organizations outside your business?

We know that, as an owner, you have worked hard for a long period of time. You have in fact already created a "legacy" even if you have never called it that. We also know that the more intentional you are about your legacy, the richer and more meaningful your transition will be from owner to the next stage in your life.

You might want to discuss what your trusted advisor(s) sees as your current and potential legacy, and how your transition plans can help support and grow what you have already done outside of work. We also urge you to talk directly with your family and friends and ask them the same question.

Then ask yourself: Is there something more I can do to help ensure my legacy? Most business owners we know who have made successful transitions look back ten or even twenty years later and rarely identify personal wealth as their most important legacy. They often point to significant relationships, time volunteering, helping someone in need, caregiving for a loved one, and other personal interactions as the most important parts of their legacy.

When business owners come to our breakfasts to tell their stories of what they did "after work," they often use the word "legacy" in their presentations. We are happy to share the following stories of their experiences with you.

Russ

Our first owner, Russ, owned and managed a successful CPA firm. Being an accountant, he said, made him "go by the numbers" when he was ready to transition his life. Unlike many owners we have met, Russ started transition planning earlier than most. At age fifty-three, he began fact gathering by looking at over one hundred possible areas of interest for postwork involvement—many in nonprofit or volunteer, faith-based organizations.

By age fifty-four, using a systematic method of gathering firsthand experience through visits and interviews, the list had been narrowed down to his top five areas of interest. He visited each organization and did in-depth interviews with leaders and employees to see where his interests and passions, as well as his accounting, financial, and entrepreneurial experiences, could best be put to work.

Then, at age fifty-five, he turned over leadership and ownership to a qualified successor and stepped into a new, partially paid leadership role in a regional private K–12 school. While doing this, he also began mentoring new business start-ups through a community college program not far from his home.

Now two years from the transition, Russ says, "I feel for the first time like I am creating a legacy. My new responsibilities are very satisfying although time demanding. There is a third area of future interest that I have put on hold until more balance and time is available."

Russ is very engaged, finding life after work very meaningful. And he is building his legacy.

Chris

Chris was the founder and owner of two family businesses when he experienced a series of events that signaled the need to move away from full-time work. An attempt to sell one business to a private equity group failed at the eleventh hour. However, the other business was growing profitably.

Then new health challenges for Chris's wife accelerated timing for his transition planning. While their three children were not involved in the businesses, all had a strong interest in how their parent's transition plans would reward their life of hard work. One of their daughters needed continued care, and any transition plan Chris developed needed to take her situation into consideration.

Chris told the breakfast group that while he was not ready to totally step away from either business, he definitely needed time to care for his wife and a daughter with special needs. Chris was also active in a number of community volunteer organizations where he wanted to spend more time but couldn't.

After getting help from a trusted advisor, Chris was able to gather the information he needed to make a transition and a decision for his legacy. All family members and owners were interviewed to gain independent perspectives of the two businesses and to develop their professional and personal visions for the future. Work was completed and summarized by trusted advisors for estate, financial, tax, and trust matters. Then all of this was reviewed by the family.

A family council meeting was subsequently held with all family members, including spouses, for all to share their opinions and personal intentions regarding the two family-owned businesses. The family meeting identified agreement on succession plans for the companies, retirement rewards for Chris, care for the special-needs daughter, independent careers for all the children and spouses, and succession planning needed for both companies. These decisions freed Chris up to pursue a personal legacy with his family as his priority.

A year later, a life trust for the special-needs daughter was established with caregiving authority given to parents, brothers, and spouses. Chris and his wife have left both companies and are now more active in their community and with social entrepreneur projects through their church.

Chris is now building his family legacy.

Dorothea

In spite of founding, building, and managing a very profitable customer service franchise business, Dorothea never felt her life was complete just by making money and being a responsible business owner. She valued her faith and community work very highly, but because of business demands, she was always torn by the lack of time she could spend on worthwhile causes.

When it was time to sell her business, she did everything right. She invested in good consulting help, valued her business based on what she would actually need to maintain a good quality of life for years to come, took a six-month sabbatical to organize a long-term personal and strategic business plan, and had two unexpected illnesses that delayed, but never stopped, her transition planning. Part of her planning included coming to the monthly transition breakfasts and always asking pertinent questions of many of the owners you have met in this book.

But it was a week-long church mission trip that helped Dorothea finally focus her legacy priorities and use many of the skills she had acquired as a successful business owner. She had gone to Guatemala to help build houses when she met Maria, an ambitious Guatemalan woman. Maria had started a "microloan program" directed at women who were small business owners. Maria's vision and actions had grown in six short years from a small, nonprofit neighborhood base to a national program.

Dorothea presented at the breakfast and described Maria: She was in her fifties and a struggling potter who needed an efficient kiln to make money to support her family. She was lucky to find a benefactor who believed in her and her work.

When her pottery business became successful, she was able to pay back the benefactor with interest. She wondered why banks couldn't make the same kinds of low-risk, small loans to other women entrepreneurs. With her own story as an example, Maria was able to convince a few banks to extend some loan capital to the nonprofit she started, and she began to screen women who had business ideas and the experience of producing products like handmade clothing, arts and crafts, and pottery. Long story short—95 percent of these loans were paid back with interest, and many of the businesses that were started are now thriving and helping the nonprofit grow each year.

Maria asked Dorothea if she was interested in using her franchising expertise to help set up and promote microloan program program offices throughout Central America. As Dorothea shared this story, you could literally see her enthusiasm building and her passion emerging. She had found her calling—and her legacy.

When Dorothea met with her transition and business sale consultants, they included a plan for financing ten years of travel for Dorothea's quarterly trips to Central America, so she could work with Maria on expanding the microloan program. Dorothea would do training for new "franchise" loan agencies in different countries and also help raise funds from banks. It turned out that the company that helped Maria value and then sell her own company made an independent and substantial contribution to the microloan program.

Dorothea is now building her legacy.

Jack

Jack was a third-generation business owner. He believed in the concept of giving back, and when it came time to transition, he had more than enough money to live comfortably and to also leave to his children. When Jack came to the breakfast, he had just established a family foundation. He was really excited to tell the group how this came about.

He said a family council identified concerns that Jack, his wife, and the next generation had for being good stewards of the abundance they were creating in their business and personal assets. Recurring family council meetings every half year identified other needs for more structured and easily managed philanthropic giving.

Significant assets that had been accumulated over the years in a life insurance policy were no longer needed to assure continuity in family ownership. So the family decided to gift these assets to a donor-advised foundation, which would then be directed by the family to make contributions to different faith-based entities. This allowed the family to become even closer, because they shared the same faith-based values and wanted to support one another in making them actionable.

In talking with his accountants and lawyers, Jack learned that a private family foundation requires ongoing monitoring and administration. There are also specific rules about taxes and other regulations that need to be explained. Experts presented this information to the entire family, and they spent a considerable amount of time discussing all the foundation issues in their family councils. When they were ready, the entire family decided to use a donor-advised foundation to handle their philanthropic contributions.

Jack told our breakfast group, "This made us not only a successful business family but also a successful philanthropic family. Setting up a foundation with clear criteria for grants and an application process took pressure off of any individual in the family and made everyone more at ease with disbursing family wealth. It also gave younger family members an opportunity to participate in a meaningful endeavor and become familiar with charitable goals, intentions, and good business management. I can say, without a doubt, that our family foundation is an enjoyable, meaningful endeavor for the entire family." Jack and his family are building their legacy.

If you are thinking about setting up a family foundation as part of your transition, there are two important questions to answer:

1. Will your foundation seek contributions from the public or be funded by one family?

2. Does your family wish to retain principal control?

Jon Gordon in his weekly newsletter on positive strategies to fuel your life and career, says there are 4 ways to leave a legacy:

1. **A Legacy of Excellence -** Saint Francis of Assisi said, "It's no use walking anywhere to preach unless your preaching is your walking." To leave a legacy of excellence, strive to be your best every day.

2. **A Legacy of Encouragement -** You have a choice. You can lift others up or bring them down. Twenty years from now when people think of you what do you want them to remember? The way you encouraged them or discouraged them?

3. **A Legacy of Purpose -** People are most energized when they are using their strengths and talents for a purpose beyond themselves. To leave a legacy of purpose, make your life about something bigger than you.

4. **A Legacy of Love -** I often think about my Mom, who passed away four years ago, and when I think about her I don't recall her faults and mistakes or the disagreements we had. After all, who is perfect? But what I remember most about her was her love for me. She gave me a legacy of love that I now share with others. Share a legacy of love and it will embrace generations to come.

www.jongordon.com

Reflecting on these stories and others you might know from friends and colleagues can help you set your own "legacy priorities." How you would like to be remembered will actually help you be intentional about actions you can take to make your legacy happen. Wanting to start the third act of your life with something fun and meaningful can also be an impetus to get your transition started.

 Three questions to ponder

1. How do you want to be remembered?

2. What activity causes you to lose track of time because you are so absorbed?

3. Where can you apply the wisdom and experience you've gained in your life?

✳ ✳ ✳

8

Avoiding Reinventing the Transition Wheel: Use "Best Practice" Examples

Don't try to reinvent the wheel—just work on making it better than anyone else.

David A. Stuebe

One of our favorite breakfast participant owners, Garvey, likes to tell the story of how he "flunked retirement." He owned a successful insurance agency and found out, after he sold it, that he was not ready to stop working. Garvey clearly admits that his "do-it-yourself" approach to transition ended up costing him valuable time and money. As most of us do, he needed help at an important time in his life. This is one universal lesson that we can all take from these transition stories.

Create a General Transition Checklist

As a business owner, you probably have an estate plan or will, own life insurance, and have given some personal thought to your retirement/"refirement." Nevertheless, in our experience, important earlier steps in transition may have been addressed insufficiently. In light of all the owner stories we have presented, to proceed with a transition plan that has high success without stressful drama or mistakes, you need thoughtful, documented input for each of the following important areas. Make sure you can put a check mark beside each one and answer with a strong yes.

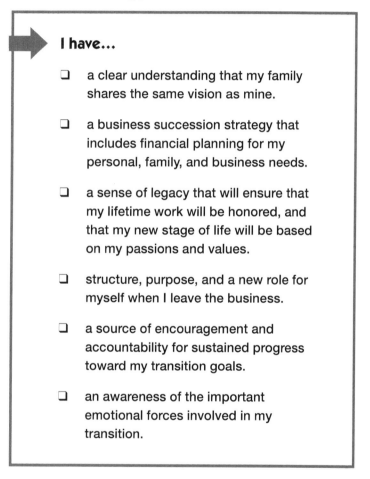

I have...

❏ a clear understanding that my family shares the same vision as mine.

❏ a business succession strategy that includes financial planning for my personal, family, and business needs.

❏ a sense of legacy that will ensure that my lifetime work will be honored, and that my new stage of life will be based on my passions and values.

❏ structure, purpose, and a new role for myself when I leave the business.

❏ a source of encouragement and accountability for sustained progress toward my transition goals.

❏ an awareness of the important emotional forces involved in my transition.

If you could not put a strong check mark beside each of the above statements, you probably need more tangible succession help.

Being Proactive, Not Reactive

We also know from experience that just "hanging on" is not going to be helpful for you or the new owner(s) of your business. Recent business research shows that when an owner is involved in a personal transition, he or she makes the decision to proceed on a new path based primarily on emotional factors, not business ones. So if you are not taking action on your transition, look to yourself to determine what is holding you up.

> **If you are not taking action on your transition, look to yourself to determine what is holding you up.**

There are a number of ways you can create an "accountability system" for yourself and your transition. First, you need to tell people close to you what you are committed to doing in your transition. We like to say, "If you say it, you can do it." As confidence grows in your transition steps, talk about it. If you are willing to communicate your plan to others—particularly family or business associates and successors—this is strong evidence that you are making change happen, and it is a good way to progress toward your transition goals.

Seeking Feedback

Feedback on your transition is essential. Your transition plan could also include an advisory board that includes your trusted advisor. This will help you with objectivity and experience. This essential feedback will:

- **affirm that you have a sound foundation.**

- **help you know if you are on track.**

- **indicate whether you have looked at enough options to clearly see the best path forward.**

- **include an alternative in case the preferred option doesn't work.**

- **provide reinforcement to change the plan when evidence shows it isn't working.**

Take Time Away from Work

Next, schedule more time away from your work—minisabbaticals, so to speak. You need to personally model accountability for transition. If you have a vacation home, put regular days on your work calendar showing your time there. Plan to take longer trips to conventions and trade shows. Go on long cruises. Sign up for minicourses. Learn a new skill. Plan to meet regularly with personal and family advisors outside of the company. Make it clear to them that the next chapter of your life will not center exclusively on your business. Keep your time lines logical and flexible. Make changes to timing based on early results.

According to Bloomberg Business Week, the key reason people look to reinvent things is that they don't know what's already been done. Ignorance, one way or another, is the leading cause of wasted effort everywhere. People who don't spend time studying the problems they're trying to solve are bound to reinvent something, and likely not nearly as well. There are only so many ways to design a website, a marketing campaign, or even a product strategy. Instead of driving minions into further brainstorming sessions, it would be wise to ask: Who else has tried to solve this problem? Can we learn from what they have done?

Making Transition a Destination

Many of you could live another twenty to thirty years after you have sold or stepped away from your business. It seems like a "no-brainer" to invest resources and make that time as productive as possible. By making a significant investment of time and money in your transition, you are proving to yourself and others that you are committed to making this transition work. If you don't commit precious resources, odds are that you will put off making real progress.

Here are some specific elements of a well-defined "destination for transition." This seven-dimension checklist addresses the key elements of a sound transition plan:

- **Family communication leads to agreements for the future of the business.**

- **Long-term ownership vision and purpose drives the business plan.**

- **Business succession is clear if the business will not be sold to outside owners and management is in place that could continue to serve under the next generation of family owners.** (A business that is not dependent on its founder is more valuable.)

- **Wealth planning encompasses business, personal, and broader family needs.**

- **Lifestyle pursuits and new areas of learning are considered for the next stage of life.**

- **Community involvement and a legacy exist beyond your company.**

- **Personal resources need to be invested in the transition planning and execution.**

Some of Our Best Advice

Our experience clearly shows that while no two transitions are identical, most owner transitions typically take five years and can run to ten or more years if internal successor development and seller financing are being used. This reality points to further steps that can focus and sustain your progress over the long haul. Here is a list of things you can do yourself to make your transition smoother:

- **Every week, schedule time for thinking about transition, and schedule it when your energy is best.**

- **Think and work regularly on your transition using the time line you have constructed.**

- **Commit significant blocks of high-quality time, not just leftover minutes.**

- **Make your plan so personal and unique that it wouldn't fit anyone else's life.**

- **Put a top priority on keeping a fresh and current detailed plan.** For encouragement, update your plan every year and reflect on its progress.

- **Get input from people who have gone ahead of you in transition.**

- **Meet at least once each month with other business owners who are further along the journey and willing to share their experiences.** These owners-in-transition round table discussions are extremely effective for providing encouragement and new ideas to owners getting started. They also encourage sustained progress for the transition journey.

Create an Accountability System for Yourself

Lack of accountability in following through with transition decisions is one of the most important actions that make transitions fail. Life happens, the business changes, you feel unsure about the next steps—all of these can derail the best transition plans.

Here are seven actions you can take to keep on track and be accountable to yourself, your family, your business associates, and your community:

1. **Commit a regular time for reviewing your progress (at least annually) on different stages of your transition.** Schedule quarterly or annual progress reviews with your advisor and advisory council. This will remind you of next steps and of your responsibility for continuing action.

2. **Plan an annual review with financial and legal advisors, and involve family in a structured annual meeting.**

3. **Budget your funds to obtain quality help for doing work that you can't do yourself.** In the same way you commit money to an IRA, SEP, or 401(k) plan, invest in specialized help that will yield dividends from proven transition expertise and put that into practice for your benefit.

4. **Organize your overall transition plan into the major steps we have presented in this book (telling your story, picking a successor, etc.).** These steps can be reviewed and updated separately. Include estate plans that reflect expected tax law changes every year, business valuation updates reflected in buy-sell documents, successor development adjusted to accommodate progress and strengths, updated wealth management plans, and business growth plans reflecting current and expected economic conditions. When change becomes visible and measurable, this is evidence that transition is working. Ask for feedback from key managers about your changed work schedule. Ask if they see you letting go and helping the next generation step into new leadership roles.

5. **Be regularly involved in extra activities outside of work, such as charitable interests, community involvement, and leadership roles for volunteer organizations.**

6. **Learn new skills. Pick up a long-deferred hobby.** Your emerging new experiences will begin to influence wealth management, charitable giving, and lifestyle decisions.

7. **Spend more time doing things with family and friends.**

Three questions to ponder

1. Who is your "go-to" advisor for your transition?

2. What schedule are you following to track activity and follow-ups?

3. Who else is part of your transition team?

In the following epilogue, we will focus on the most important lessons we have learned in our transition work:

Your need to take control and act on your transition NOW!

✳ ✳ ✳

EPILOGUE
Taking Control of Your Transition—With a Little Help from Your Friends!

You can't connect the dots looking forward; you can only connect them looking backward. So you have to trust that the dots will somehow connect in your future. You have to trust in something—your gut, destiny, life, karma, whatever. This approach has never let me down, and it has made all the difference in my life.

Steve Jobs

We conclude by reminding you about our "three transition truths" from Chapter One:

1. **Find the courage to personally tell your business story.**

2. **Develop a vision of the future for yourself and your company.**

3. **Be a clear communicator of the future.**

If you have done these three things, you are ready to continue on your transition journey.

A Sequential Framework for Business Transitions

Legacy

Lifestyle

Financial

Business

Successor

Ownership

A Five Year Process?

You have now heard many owners talk personally about the details of their transition stories. The graphic above shows the logical sequence that we have seen during our years in the "transition business" and we urge you to consider covering each one of these components as you plan your own transition.

We also know that because every transition is unique, many of you will not need to spend equal amounts of time on each transition step. But going forward, you should be aware that the process will most likely take longer than you expected and you probably will need some professional and trusted help along the way.

Mapping Out Your Transition

"What's next for me?" is a common question among today's business owners and leaders. The key to mapping a productive experience in any transition is to identify the next stage in your life and work.

Based on the experiences you have read about from owners like yourselves and other professionals who write about transitions, we have found six dimensions of life that can help you create a comprehensive transition map:

1. **Ownership.** Involve your family in the transition decision and consider their needs.

   Action Steps: Form a family council, hold family meetings, and engage in long-range planning.

2. **Successor.** Evaluate internal candidates and/or conduct an external search.

   Action Steps: Plan to transfer leadership and inform key stakeholders of your decision.

3. **Business.** Assess your business's readiness for transition by evaluating its stability and predictable cash flow.

   Action Steps: Develop long-term business plans with timing and budgets.

4. **Financial.** Balance wealth management with succession planning to meet family lifestyle needs going forward.

   Action Steps: Obtain a business valuation, develop a buy-sell agreement, get tax-planning assistance, and plan your charitable giving.

5. **Lifestyle.** When planning how to spend your time and energy after the transition, focus on your passions.

   Action Steps: Determine your core values and passions.

6. **Legacy.** Leave a legacy by giving back. You can start giving back today, rather than waiting until you are ready for a more formal transition.

   Action Steps: Consider various ways to support the charities and causes you are most passionate about, including financial contributions and volunteer opportunities.

Looking at our graphic on page 92, you can see that a logical sequence of components exists in a successful transition. We urge you to consider covering each one of these as you plan. Note that every transition is unique, and you will probably not need to spend equal amounts of time on each step. Some steps may only take a few months, and some could take a year or two. Life happens, so be prepared!

> **Every transition is unique and you will probably not need to spend equal amounts of time on each step.**

Now it is up to you! Nobody can force you to make a transition. We hope that you were able to connect and identify with some of the stories of the owners in this book—they all had courage, and none of them experienced completely smooth sailing. But they all pursued and are pursuing a vision they created with the help of family, friends, business colleagues, and trusted advisors. We are confident that you can do the same!

And if you happen to be in the Twin Cities area in the future and are hungry for good stories, good company, and a good meal, we welcome you to join us for our monthly transition breakfast and to contribute to the growing legacy of so many successful owners who are telling their stories.

* * *

AFTERWORD

Learn about Biz-Bridge.com

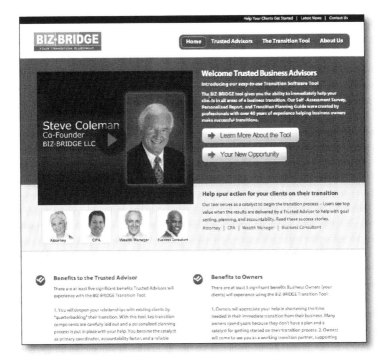

Finally, we also want to introduce you to a software transition tool we have developed for you and your trusted advisor(s) that incorporates the six elements on the chart above and ten key components to a successful transition: Biz-Bridge (www.Biz-Bridge.com).

Here's How It Works

Your trusted advisor will be the person who needs to provide you with the Biz-Bridge tool. Simply ask him or her to go to the website above and become a licensed member of the Biz-Bridge transition community of professional advisors.

Your advisor will then send you an electronic thirty-statement transition survey that you can complete on your computer. There is no proprietary information that you will be sharing, and it will take you only about fifteen minutes to complete. When you are finished, hit submit, and your advisor will receive your answers, a detailed nineteen-page personalized report, and a transition-planning guide to help you begin or complete your business transition.

You will work with your advisor using the planning guide we have provided and thus begin your exciting transition journey.

You will see that the ten key transition components that we have identified in this book are included in your personalized report. We will also indicate whether you are dreaming about, worrying about, or actively pursuing a transition path. Biz-Bridge materials highlight the differences your transition path might take if you are a family-owned or an otherwise privately owned company.

The real intent of the Biz-Bridge software tool is to help you get started or take you to the next level in your transition. In any case, it is our intent to help you take control of your transition and be held accountable for making regular progress each year with the help of your trusted advisor.

✳ ✳ ✳

About the Authors

Steve Coleman
Partner, The Platinum Group and
President of Biz-Bridge LLC

Writing this book has been a labor of love. I'm a business guy. It all started as a kid selling strawberries, corn and apples from a roadside table. After school and 15 years of working in big corporations, I changed gears to become an advisor to small and growing business owners. Since the early 1980s, I've been sharing my experiences and war stories with family and privately-owned companies. There have been hundreds of businesses served, but no two are the same. Owners want to grow, enter new markets, add products and services, apply new technology, and reach customers through new distribution channels. I've learned that privately-held businesses are the backbone of the American economy.

I hope that the stories in this book will alert, inform, challenge, and provoke owners into action; and that families, partnerships, businesses, and communities will be preserved and strengthened. That's why *Find What's NEXT For You* is my true passion and a gift to business owners and their advisors.

James Gambone
**Partner, Points Of View Incorporated
and Chief Information Officer of
Biz-Bridge, LLC**

For the past 22 years, a significant focus of my consulting work and writing has been to help generations better understand and cooperate with each other. Almost every business transition requires a generational transfer. In most of the breakfast discussions we have had over the past eight years, generational and intergenerational issues have surfaced. I am excited that this book now offers a new platform to present and challenge owners to deal with the differences between themselves and a new generation of owners.

As a business owner and entrepreneur myself, I know how difficult it is to step back from the business and try to look calmly into the future. Coming from an Italian family restaurant business, I understand that sometimes it is difficult to ask for help. However, listening to owners tell their transition stories has been a valuable education for me and the companies I am involved in.

I also know from many years as a part-time graduate professor, clear communication and having a realistic plan for the future are the two most important factors for success in almost any venture. I sincerely hope that I have helped to clearly communicate these two critical lessons in this book.

✳ ✳ ✳

– Notes –

32104592R00060

Made in the USA
Charleston, SC
08 August 2014